11-88

ISAAC ASIMOV'S
Library of the Universe

Ancient Astronomy

by Isaac Asimov

Gareth Stevens Publishing
Milwaukee

The reproduction rights to all photographs and illustrations in this book are controlled by the individuals or institutions credited on page 32 and may not be reproduced without their permission.

Library of Congress Cataloging-in-Publication Data

Asimov, Isaac, 1920-
    Ancient astronomy / by Isaac Asimov. -- A Gareth Stevens children's books ed.
        p.   cm. -- (Isaac Asimov's library of the universe)
    Bibliography: p.
    Includes index.
    Summary: Briefly describes beliefs of astronomers from ancient times to 1609,
when Galileo's discoveries through the telescope gave birth to modern astronomy.
    ISBN 1-555-32393-6.   ISBN 1-555-32368-5 (lib. bdg.)
    1. Astronomy, Ancient -- Juvenile literature.   [1. Astronomy, Ancient.]   I. Title.   II.
Series: Asimov, Isaac, 1920-   Library of the universe.
QB16.A75   1988
520'.9'01—dc19   88-17564

A Gareth Stevens Children's Books edition

Edited, designed, and produced by
Gareth Stevens, Inc.   7317 West Green Tree Road   Milwaukee, Wisconsin 53223, USA

Cover: © M. Timothy O'Keefe/Tom Stack and Associates
Designer: Laurie Shock
Picture research: Kathy Keller
Artwork commissioning: Kathy Keller and Laurie Shock
Project editor: Mark Sachner
Research editor: Scott Enk
Technical advisers and consulting editors: Greg Walz-Chojnacki and Francis Reddy

1 2 3 4 5 6 7 8 9 94 93 92 91 90 89

CONTENTS

Nowadays, we have seen planets up close, all the way to distant Uranus. We have mapped Venus through its clouds. We have seen dead volcanoes on Mars and live ones on Io, one of Jupiter's moons. We have detected strange objects no one even knew about until recently: quasars, pulsars, and black holes. We have learned amazing things about how the Universe was born, and we have some ideas about how it might die. Nothing can be more astonishing and more interesting.

But all our knowledge of the Universe started with ancient people who looked at the sky and wondered. They did not have our instruments. They had only their eyes. Even so, they managed to study the objects in the sky, to observe how they moved, and to work out reasons for that movement. Our knowledge of the Universe began with these ancient astronomers. We could not have come as far as we have without their ability to get things going.

Isaac Asimov

In Awe of the Heavens

We don't often look at the night sky.
The dust and lights of modern life
hide it. But ancient people had a
better chance to study the sky and
see the patterns, or constellations,
of the stars.

They traced out constellations
that looked like people and animals,
and made up stories to account for
their being in the sky. They noticed
that the Moon changed its shape
from night to night and changed
its position against the stars. The
earliest calendars, which showed the
change of seasons, were based on
the changes of the Moon. Ancient
priests were among the first
astronomers. They had to study the
sky carefully to make sure that the
calendars were accurate.

Ancient people were fascinated by the rhythms of
the sky. The first astronomical observations were
painted on the walls of caves.

The Astronomy of the Far East

Some stars and constellations, like the Big Dipper, always stay in the northern part of the sky. So ancient sailors used the stars to guide them. The Polynesians found their way to distant islands over the vast Pacific Ocean by watching the stars.

In China, too, astronomy was important, because changes in the sky were thought to mean future changes on Earth. The ancient Chinese astronomers watched for any new stars that might appear, as well as eclipses of the Sun and Moon, so they could warn people of future events. Two astronomers who got drunk and didn't foresee an eclipse had their heads cut off!

Left: Using their knowledge of the sea and sky, Polynesian sailors crossed the vast Pacific Ocean in fragile boats.

Below: the compass — one of China's many scientific firsts.

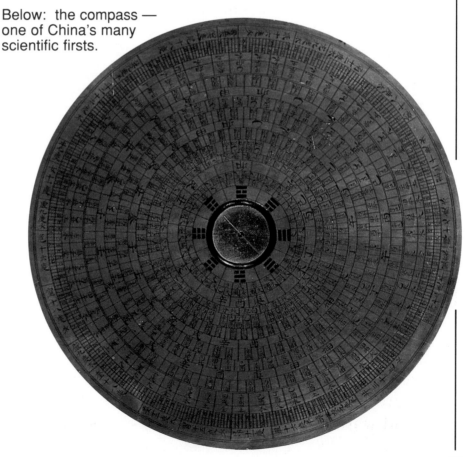

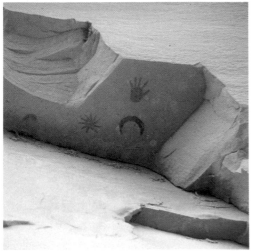

Above: an early American observatory,
the Caracol of Chichen Itza (chee-CHEN
eet-SAH), an ancient Mayan city of Yucatán,
Mexico. A thousand years ago, Mayans
studied the movement of the planet Venus
through openings in the tower's top.

Left: a sketch of the Moon? Anasazi Indians
drew this on the rocks of New Mexico's
Chaco Canyon.

Early American Astronomy

The Mayans (pronounced MY-ans), who lived in southern Mexico, developed a written language and a clever way of writing numbers. They watched the movements of the Moon and the planet Venus carefully. By about the year AD 800, they had worked out a calendar that was more accurate than the one being used in Europe at the time!

They also learned to use the movements of the Moon and Sun to predict eclipses. And they may have built special buildings called observatories to study the sky. But their civilization declined after 900. When the Spaniards arrived soon after 1500, most Mayan records were destroyed.

An Aztec astronomer. The Aztec Indians were the most powerful group in Mexico when Spanish adventurers arrived.

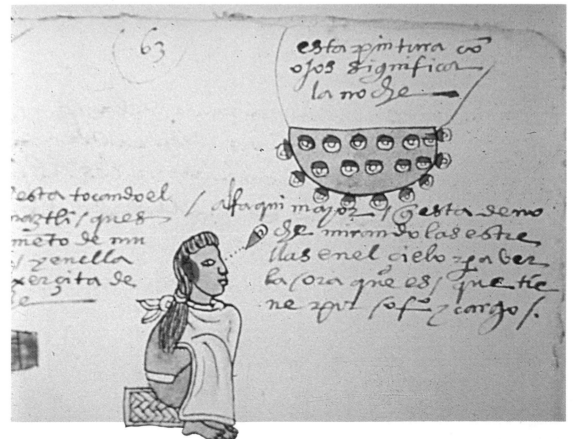

The Sky-watchers of Egypt

The ancient Egyptians' (ee-GYP-shuns) very lives depended on the Nile River. When the river flooded their fields, it made it possible for the Egyptians to grow their crops.

Their priests carefully recorded when the floods came, and found that they came about every 365 days. So the Egyptians were the first to use a calendar with a 365-day year. They also noticed that the bright star Sirius rose with the Sun when the flood was due. They also invented sundials to measure the time of day by the movement of the Sun. But otherwise, the ancient Egyptians weren't much interested in astronomy.

Sirius, the brightest star in the sky.

Left: Over 4,000 years ago, Egyptians used the position of Sirius to predict the annual flooding of the Nile.

Now you see 'em more, now you see 'em less

Some stars, called variable stars, seem to get slightly brighter and dimmer. Why do these stars change in brightness? Some are double stars, and their brightness varies as one member of the pair eclipses, or blocks, the other. Ancient star-watchers, such as the Arabs, might have seen such changes, but no one mentioned them. Why not? The ancients seemed to believe that the heavens never changed, so maybe no one wanted to admit stars could vary in brightness!

Babylon — The Cradle of Western Astronomy

The ancient Babylonians (bab-ill-O-nee-ans) were the first to study the movements of the planets Mercury, Venus, Mars, Jupiter, and Saturn. These planets follow complicated paths against the stars.

The Babylonians kept detailed records of these paths and learned to predict them. Like all ancient peoples, they believed that studying planetary movements gave hints as to future happenings on Earth.

Left: an ancient observatory? One Biblical story tells how the people of a Babylonian city tried to build a stairway to the stars — the Tower of Babel.

Below: This Babylonian view of the Universe shows a disk of land with water surrounding everything. Babylonia is shown at the center of the disk.

The ancient Greek philosopher Pythagoras. His followers were skilled in mathematics and astronomy. They were among the first to think of the Earth as a huge ball.

The Astronomers of Greece

The earliest Greek astronomers probably picked up most of their knowledge from the Babylonians. The Greek philosopher Thales (THA-leez) predicted an eclipse of the Sun that took place in the year 585 BC. And if the stories are true, Thales most likely used Babylonian methods.

Around 550 BC, the philosopher Pythagoras (pih-THAG-er-us) pointed out that the Evening Star and the Morning Star were really the same body. Today, we know that this body is the planet Venus. Pythagoras, too, probably used the knowledge of the Babylonians.

But then the ancient Greek astronomers moved ahead. Most people back then thought that the Earth was flat, but some Greek astronomers thought that it might have the shape of a ball. Others thought that the light of the Moon was really reflected sunlight.

Today, we know how right they were!

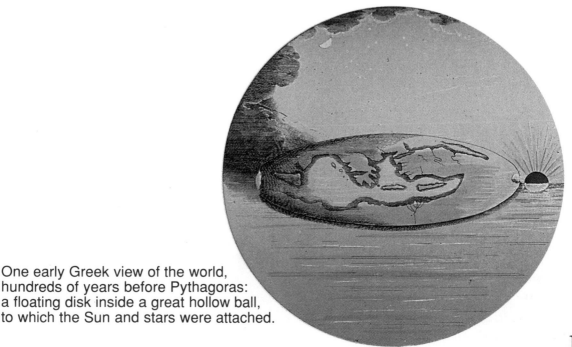

One early Greek view of the world, hundreds of years before Pythagoras: a floating disk inside a great hollow ball, to which the Sun and stars were attached.

Understanding the Heavenly Motions

To the Greeks, the Earth was a huge ball at the center of the Universe, and the objects in the sky moved around it in great circles. Each planet moved in a separate circle. The Moon was lowest. Then came Mercury, Venus, the Sun, Mars, Jupiter, and Saturn. The stars were farthest out.

Ptolemy at work in his Egyptian observatory.

Below: Ptolemy thought that the Sun, Moon, and planets circled Earth.

To explain why the planets changed direction, two astronomers, Hipparchus (hip-AR-kus) and Ptolemy (TOL-em-ee), worked out a detailed scheme of the planetary motions. Ptolemy did his work in about AD 150. But he used the work of Hipparchus from about 130 BC. So it took a long time — about 280 years — and a lot of work to come up with the scheme. It was extremely complicated, but it could be used to work out future positions of the planets.

Much of Ptolemy's work is based on that of Hipparchus, a Greek astronomer who lived over 200 years earlier.

The world's first star map — just a case of mistaken identity?

Hipparchus was the first astronomer ever to make a star map. According to reports, he spotted a new star in 134 BC. He then went ahead and made a star map to help identify further sightings. But did he really see a new star? His original reports were destroyed, and we have no record anywhere else of such a star. Not even the Chinese reported it! Should we thank a case of mistaken identity for the first star map? We might never know!

Measuring Earth

So the ancient Greeks believed that Earth was a ball. But just how large was Earth's ball — and how distant were the planets?

In about 240 BC, a Greek astronomer in Egypt, Eratosthenes (air-ah-TOS-then-eez), made an exciting discovery. He found that when the Sun was directly overhead in one city, it cast a shadow in another city, 500 miles (800 km) to the north.

Eratosthenes figured that this meant Earth's surface curved. He also figured out that Earth was a ball about 25,000 miles (40,000 km) around. Today, we know he was right.

Hipparchus later studied Earth's shadow when it eclipsed the Moon. From the size of the Moon, he decided it must be about 240,000 miles (384,000 km) from Earth. He was right about that, too!

Right: By combining his observations with his skill in mathematics, Eratosthenes measured Earth's size and the Moon's distance.

The Arabs — Bringing Light to the Dark Ages

After Ptolemy, Greek science faded and Europe slowly
entered a Dark Age. But the Arabs, beginning in AD 632,
set up a large empire, discovered Greek books on science and
mathematics, translated them into Arabic, and studied them.

In some cases, they even improved on the Greeks. In about
900, an Arab named Al-Battani (al-bat-AH-nee) worked out
new ways of figuring out planetary positions.

In about 1150, Europeans began to translate the Arabic
versions of the Greek books into Latin. If it hadn't been for
the Arabs, Greek science might have been totally lost!

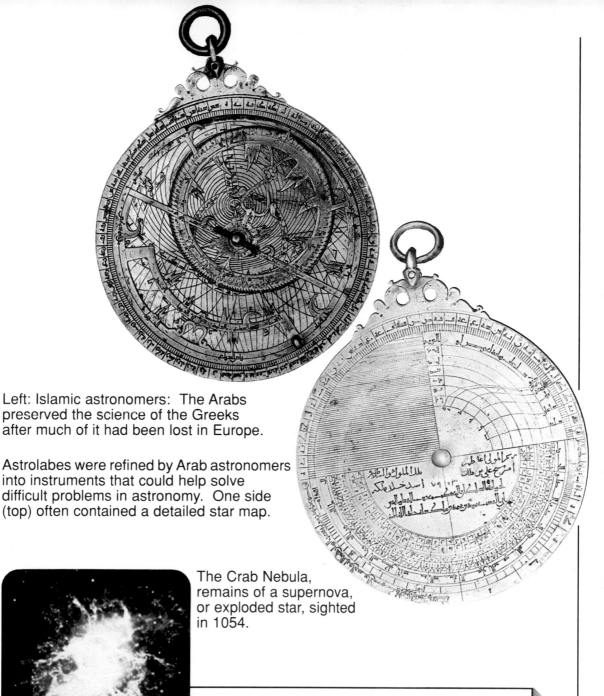

Left: Islamic astronomers: The Arabs preserved the science of the Greeks after much of it had been lost in Europe.

Astrolabes were refined by Arab astronomers into instruments that could help solve difficult problems in astronomy. One side (top) often contained a detailed star map.

The Crab Nebula, remains of a supernova, or exploded star, sighted in 1054.

The Dark Ages — they weren't dark everywhere!

In July 1054, a star blazed out in the heavens. For three weeks, it was so bright it could be seen in daylight. At night, it cast a dim shadow. But Europeans in the Dark Ages were so uninterested in astronomy that no one there seemed to notice it. The only reason we know that the star appeared was because Chinese, Arab, American Indian, and Japanese astronomers carefully noted it.

21

Nicolaus Copernicus, the Polish scientist who argued that the Sun, not Earth, was the center of the Universe (right).

Earth's Place in the Cosmos

The Greek scheme of the Universe was so complicated that other European astronomers looked for simpler methods. The Polish astronomer Copernicus (co-PER-nic-us) decided that a better scheme would be to place the Sun at the center of the Universe and have all the planets circle it.

Earth would have to circle the Sun, too. This seemed against common sense, but in 1543, Copernicus wrote that his idea would make it much easier to figure out planetary positions. For more than 50 years, astronomers argued as to whether Copernicus was right or not.

The Gum Nebula.

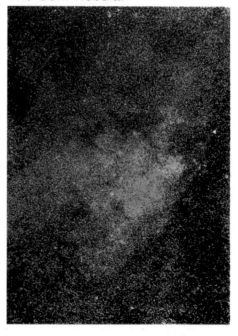

> ### Supernova — a star as bright as the Moon
>
> *Supernovas are stars that explode in a terrific blaze of light. Sometimes they leave behind a cloud of dust and gas that shows the place of the explosion. One such cloud, the Gum Nebula, might mark the explosion of a star only about 1,500 light-years away. When it was at its peak — about 11,000 years ago — this star must have shone as brightly as the full Moon. Imagine how astonished even primitive human beings must have been when they saw it!*

The Changing Views

European astronomers were beginning to find out that the Greeks were indeed wrong now and then!

In 1572, a Danish astronomer, Tycho Brahe (TY-co BRAH-hee), spotted and studied a bright new star in the sky. Eventually, it faded away. This would have been fine, but the Greeks had thought that the sky never changed.

In 1577, Tycho Brahe studied a comet and tried to figure out its distance by seeing whether it changed its position when viewed from different places. It didn't, so it had to be quite far — certainly farther than the Moon.

The Greeks had thought comets were inside our atmosphere. But all this made Europeans more ready to accept new ideas, like Copernicus's idea that Earth circled the Sun.

English astronomer
Edmund Halley.

Comets — the ancients just couldn't handle them!

Early astronomers just couldn't cope with comets. They came suddenly, moved against the stars unpredictably, and then vanished. People thought they might be special warnings of disaster, and so they panicked. It wasn't until 1705 that an astronomer, Edmund Halley, explained the motions of comets through space and showed that they moved about the Sun in unusual but predictable orbits. Even so, when comets appear today, some people are still frightened.

Tycho Brahe was among those who unknowingly witnessed the explosion of a star in 1572 (above). He recorded the position of the supernova so precisely that modern astronomers have found its remains (left).

Galileo experiments with his first telescope.

The Birth of Modern Astronomy

The turning point came when a telescope was invented in Holland. An Italian astronomer, Galileo (gal-ill-AY-o), heard of this, built his own, and, in 1609, pointed it at the heavens.

At once he discovered many stars too dim to see without a telescope. He also found that the Moon was a world — with craters, mountains, and what looked like seas. He found that the planet Jupiter had four moons that moved about it, and that Venus changed shape, just as the Moon did.

This didn't fit the Greek views, but it did fit Copernicus's. At that moment, modern astronomy had begun!

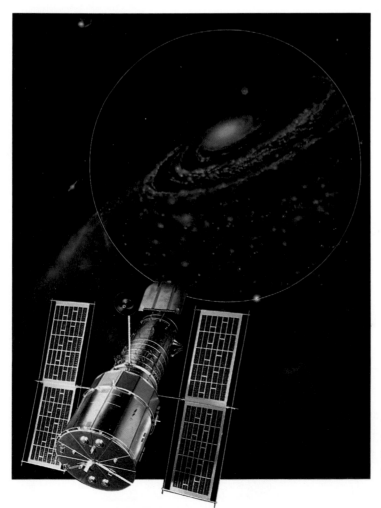

The Hubble Space Telescope will vastly improve our ability to see the Universe.

Fact File: Observing the Universe — Then and Now

The earliest observatories might have been open platforms where astronomers could watch the sky with no buildings in the way.

At least 5,000 years ago, ancient astronomers began using large stones arranged in rows or circles to chart how the Sun and stars moved through the sky. The most famous ancient observatory of this kind is a circle of large upright stones called Stonehenge, in England.

American Indians also built circles of stones lined up with the Sun and stars to figure out sunrise and the start of summer.

The famous observatory built in Egypt in about 300 BC might have had early instruments like the astrolabe. Greek and Arab astronomers used the astrolabe — which means "star-finder" — to sight the Sun, Moon, planets, and stars, predict their movements, and tell time.

Before the telescope was invented in 1609, perhaps the most advanced observatory of all was the one founded by the Danish astronomer Tycho Brahe in the late 1500s. It used long, open sights to watch the sky.

The telescope was the beginning of modern astronomy. Today, in addition to optical telescopes, astronomers have instruments to pick up radio waves from things too far away to see well. They have even sent instruments into space.

We use these instruments to learn about things that ancient astronomers never dreamed of. But, in many ways, we want to learn about the Universe for many of the same reasons the first astronomers did long ago!

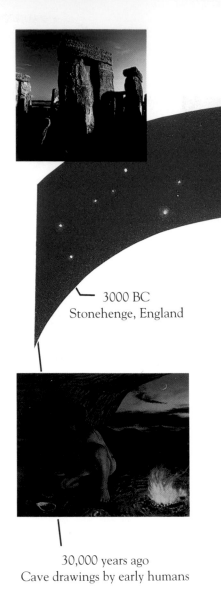

3000 BC
Stonehenge, England

30,000 years ago
Cave drawings by early humans

Above and right: We humans have stargazed longer than we have known how to write. Here is a brief sampling of observatories from prehistoric days to the present.

AD 1100
Chichen Itza, Yucatán, Mexico

AD 1000
Early American
stone alignments

1576
Tycho Brahe's observatory
Ven, Denmark

1600s
Beijing Observatory, China

1724
Delhi Observatory, India

1838
Pulkova Observatory,
Leningrad, USSR

1780s Observatory in
Quito, Equador

1967
Mauna Kea Observatory, Hawaii, USA

1990s
Hubble Space Telescope

29

More Books About Astronomy

Here are more books that contain information about astronomy. If you are interested in them, check your library or bookstore.

Astronomy Basics. Paton (Franklin Watts)
The Macmillan Book of Astronomy. Gallant (Macmillan)
Sky Watchers of Ages Past. Weiss (Houghton Mifflin)
Space Spotter's Guide. Asimov (Gareth Stevens)

Places to Visit

You can explore the same parts of the cosmos that fascinated ancient astronomers — without leaving Earth. Here are some museums and centers where you can find a variety of space exhibits.

Touch the Universe
Manitoba Planetarium
Winnipeg, Manitoba

National Air and Space Museum
Smithsonian Institution
Washington, DC

Science North Solar Observatory
Sudbury, Ontario

Andrus Planetarium
Hudson River Museum
Yonkers, New York

Henry Crown Space Center
Museum of Science and Industry
Chicago, Illinois

H. R. MacMillan Planetarium
Vancouver, British Columbia

For More Information About Astronomy

Here are some people you can write to for more information about astronomy. Be sure to tell them exactly what you want to know about or see. Remember to include your age, full name, and address.

For information about astronomy:
STARDATE
MacDonald Observatory
Austin, Texas 78712

Space Communications Branch
Ministry of State for Science and Technology
240 Sparks Street, C. D. Howe Building
Ottawa, Ontario K1A 1A1, Canada

For astro-photography:
Caltech Bookstore
California Institute of Technology
Mail Code 1-51
Pasadena, California 91125

For catalogs of slides, posters, and other astronomy materials:
AstroMedia Order Department
1027 N. 7th Street
Milwaukee, Wisconsin 53233

Sky Publishing Corporation
49 Bay State Road
Cambridge, Massachusetts 02238-1290

Glossary

annual: happening once a year.

astrolabe: "star-finder"; an instrument once used to solve complicated problems of astronomy, including the distances of the Sun and other celestial objects.

astronomy: the scientific study of the various bodies of the Universe.

atmosphere: the gases that surround some planets. Our atmosphere consists of oxygen, nitrogen, and other gases.

billion: in this book, the number represented by 1 followed by nine zeroes — 1,000,000,000. In some places, such as the United Kingdom (Britain), this number is called "a thousand million." In these places, one billion would then be represented by 1 followed by *12* zeroes — 1,000,000,000,000: a million million.

calendar: a system for dividing time, most commonly into days, weeks, and months. Every calendar has a starting day and ending day for the year.

comet: an object made of ice, rock, and gas with a vapor tail that may be seen when the comet comes near the Sun. Early people often believed comets predicted disasters.

constellations: groupings of stars in the sky that seem to trace familiar patterns or figures. Constellations are often named after the shapes they resemble.

Copernicus, Nicolaus: a Polish astronomer, the first to correctly argue that the Sun, not Earth, was the center of our Solar system and that the planets revolved around it.

Dark Ages: a popular name for the early part of the Middle Ages, a period of several hundred years that is often associated with a lack of learning throughout Europe.

Earth: the planet on which we live, the third planet from the Sun.

eclipse: when one body crosses through the shadow of another. During a solar eclipse, parts of the Earth are in the shadow of the Moon as the Moon cuts right across the Sun and hides it for a period of time.

Galileo: an Italian astronomer who developed the use of the telescope to better study the Universe.

nebula: a vast cloud of dust and gas in the Universe.

observatory: a building or site designed and equipped with scientific instruments for the study of astronomy.

philosopher: a person who studies human experience and offers ideas about how we might fit into the Universe.

planet: one of the bodies that revolve around our Sun. Earth is one of the planets.

Ptolemy: a Greek astronomer who, in about AD 150, worked out a detailed map of the planetary movements. He used the work of Hipparchus from about 130 BC.

sundial: an instrument to measure the time of day by the movement and location of the Sun.

supernova: an explosion of most of the material of a star, causing a short-lived red giant which emits great amounts of energy.

telescope: an instrument usually made of lenses or mirrors to help us see and detect distant objects.

Tower of Babel: according to the Bible, a huge tower built by people who thought they could reach the heavens by climbing higher and higher into the sky.

Index

The publishers wish to thank the following for permission to reproduce copyright material: front cover, © M. Timothy O'Keefe/Tom Stack and Associates; pp. 4-5, 28 (lower), 29 (top left), © Garret Moore, 1987; pp. 6-7, Bishop Museum; pp. 7 (lower), 14, 20, 22 (upper), 26, The Granger Collection, New York; p. 8 (upper), 29 (top center), © Frank Reddy; p. 8 (lower), United States Geological Survey; pp. 9, 23, 28 (upper), 29 (bottom left), Science Photo Library; p. 10, © Kurt Burmann, 1988; p. 11, © Frank Zullo; pp. 12-13, Kunsthistorisches Museum; p. 13 (lower right), 16 (both), 22 (lower), 29 (top right and second from top, right), Mary Evans Picture Library; pp. 15, 17, 25 (upper), Ann Ronan Picture Library; p. 19, © Mark Maxwell, 1988; p. 21 (both upper right), Adler Planetarium; p. 21 (lower left), courtesy of NASA; pp. 24, 29 (center left and second from bottom, right), photographs courtesy of Julian Baum; p. 25 (lower), National Optical Astronomy Observatories; pp. 27, 29 (bottom right), Space Telescope Science Institute; p. 29 (bottom center), © Greg Vaughn/Tom Stack and Associates.